# DIM SUM TIME

For our little dumpling Avery.
      XOXOXOXO
   -Mommy and Daddy

每週一次,爸爸和媽媽都會帶我,弟弟和姐姐去餐廳吃點心。"吃點心的時間到了!"弟弟大聲叫道。

Once a week, mommy and daddy take me, my little brother, and my big sister, to the restaurant for dim sum.

"It's Dim Sum time!" little brother yells out.

有很多點心我喜歡吃,
yǒu hěn duō diǎn xin wǒ xǐ huan chī

但有一個是我最喜
dàn yǒu yī gè shì wǒ zuì xǐ

歡的。
huan de

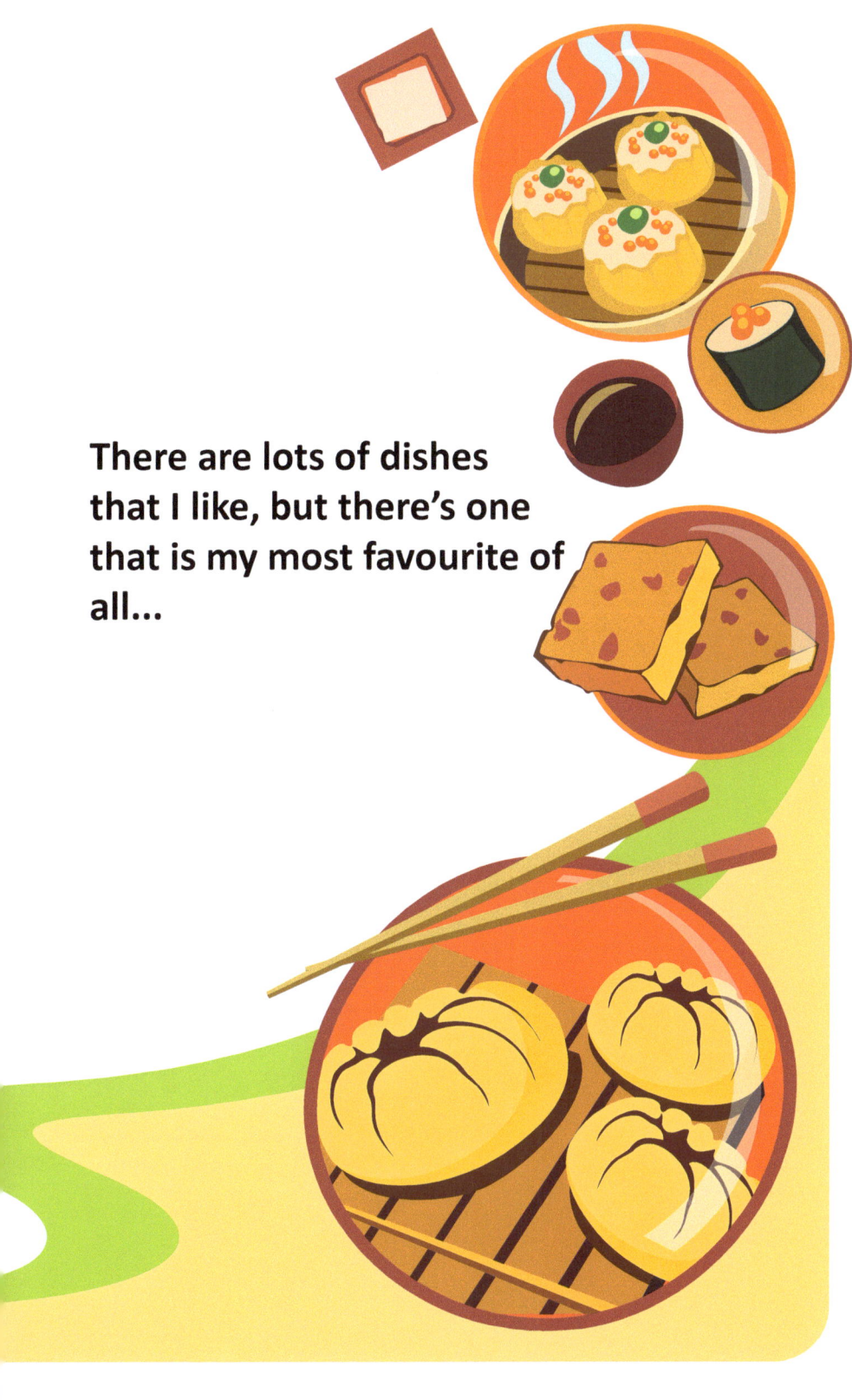

There are lots of dishes that I like, but there's one that is my most favourite of all...

"蝦餃！蝦餃！我愛蝦餃！"
xiā jiǎo　　xiā jiǎo　　wǒ ài xiā jiǎo

"安靜一點吧"媽媽說。
ān jìng yī diǎn bā　　mā ma shuì

我告訴肚子要耐心等候。
wǒ gào su dù zi yāo nài xīn děng hòu

"Har gao! Har gao! I love my Har Gao!"

"Hush," says mommy and I tell my tummy to wait.

在餐廳內,服務員推著擺滿了各款點心的小車,一路推一路叫出不同的點心。有這麼多點心,但是我的蝦餃在哪裡?

In the restaurant, carts piled high with food are pushed around while waiters call out the dishes.

There are so many dishes to choose from, but where's my Har Gao?

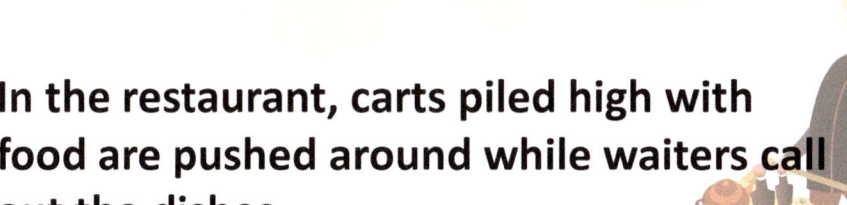

弟弟喜歡叉燒包 - 一個大麵包裡裝滿了美味的肉。

我吃了一個叉燒包,但是我的蝦餃在哪裡?

**Little brother likes Char Siu Bao - a fluffy soft bun filled with yummy meat.**

**I eat a Char Siu Bao too, but where's my Har Gao?**

姐姐吃了她喜愛的燒賣 -
jiě jie chī liǎo tā xǐ ài de shāo mài

薄皮裡有多汁的豬肉。
bó pí lǐ yǒu duō zhī de zhū ròu

我吃了一個燒賣,但是我的
wǒ chī liǎo yī gè shāo mài dàn shì wǒ de

蝦餃在哪裡?
xiā jiǎo zài nǎ lǐ

Big sister eats her Siu Mai - juicy pork wrapped in a soft pasta skin.

I eat a Siu Mai too, but where's my Har Gao?

爸爸挑選了他喜愛的鳳爪 -
甜蜜的雞爪，軟滑的皮。
我吃了一隻鳳爪，但是我的蝦餃在哪裡？

Daddy picks out his Fong Djau - sweet chicken paws with smooth and soft skin.

I eat a Fong Djau too, but where's my Har Gao?

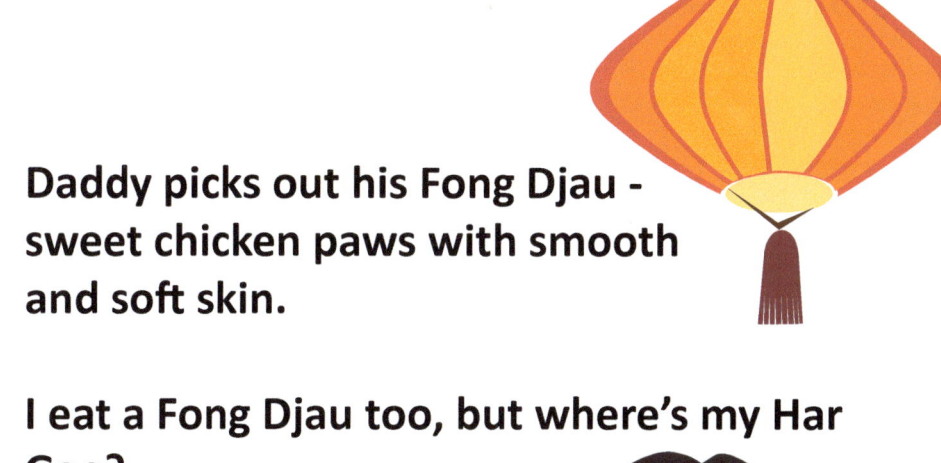

媽媽訂了一些蘿蔔糕 -
用蘿蔔和蝦煎炸的食物。
我吃了一塊蘿蔔糕,但是我的蝦餃在哪裡?

蝦餃！蝦餃！
xiā jiǎo  xiā jiǎo

我愛蝦餃
wǒ ài xiā jiǎo

Har Gao! Har Gao!
I love my Har Gao!

最後，蝦餃終於來了 - 水晶
zuì hòu xiā jiǎo zhōng yú lái liǎo shuǐ jīng

外皮裡有新鮮的大蝦。
wài pí lǐ yǒu xīn xiān de dà xiā

但是現在我的肚子
dàn shì xiàn zài wǒ de dù zi

已經太飽了。
yǐ jīng tài bǎo liǎo

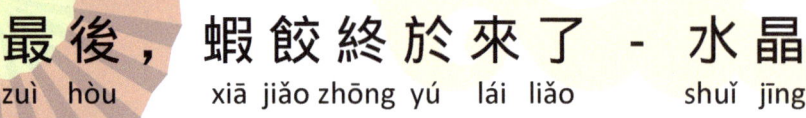

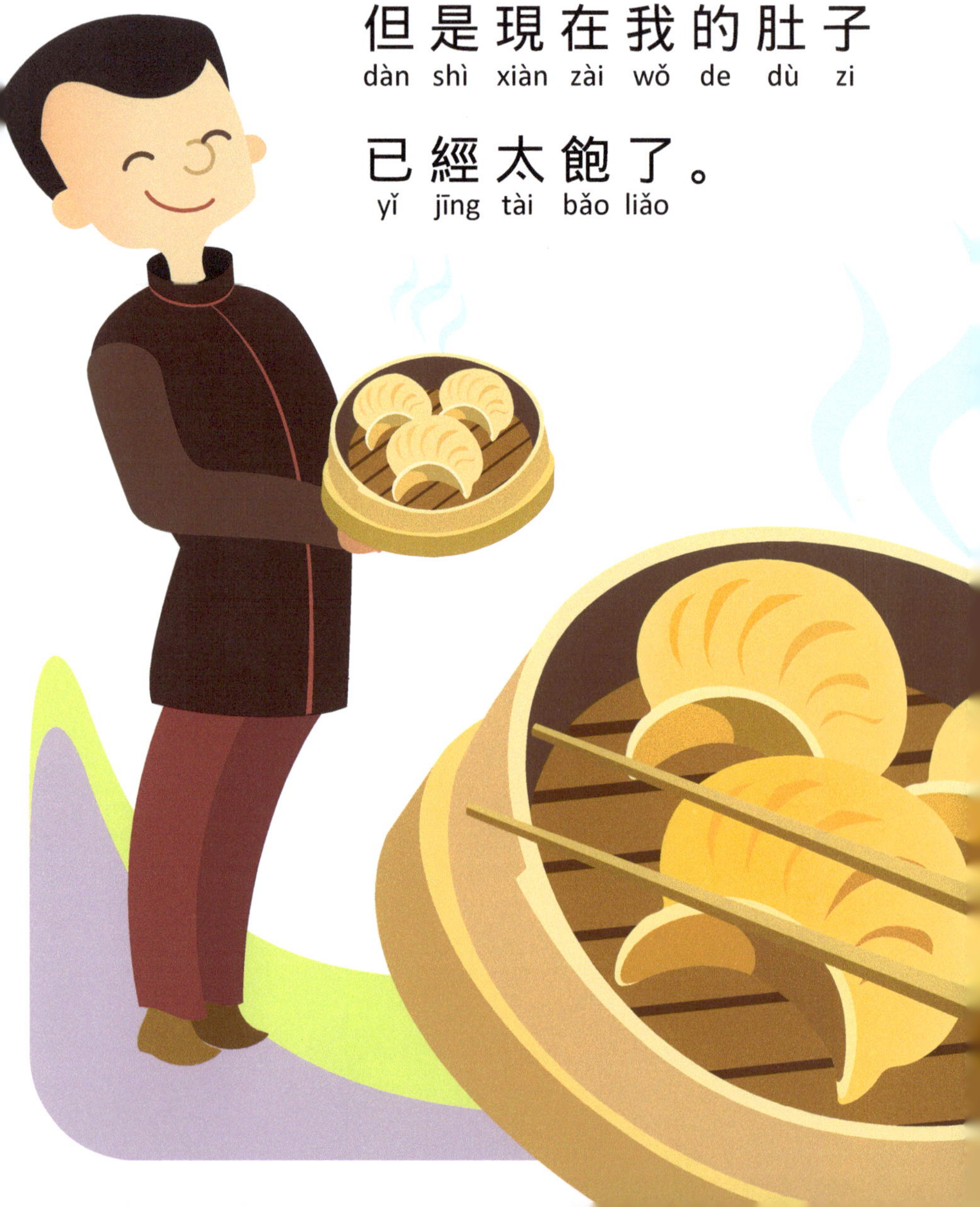

**Finally the Har Gao arrives - crystal clear dumpling skin with a big fresh shrimp inside.**

**But now my tummy is too full.**

我請服務員拿一個盒子來打
wǒ qǐng fú wù yuán ná yī gè hé zi lái dǎ

包，把蝦餃帶回家。
bāo bǎ xiā jiǎo dài huí jiā

因為我從來不喜歡
yīn wèi wǒ cóng lái bù xǐ huan

浪費食物，尤其是...
làng fèi shí wù yóu qí shì

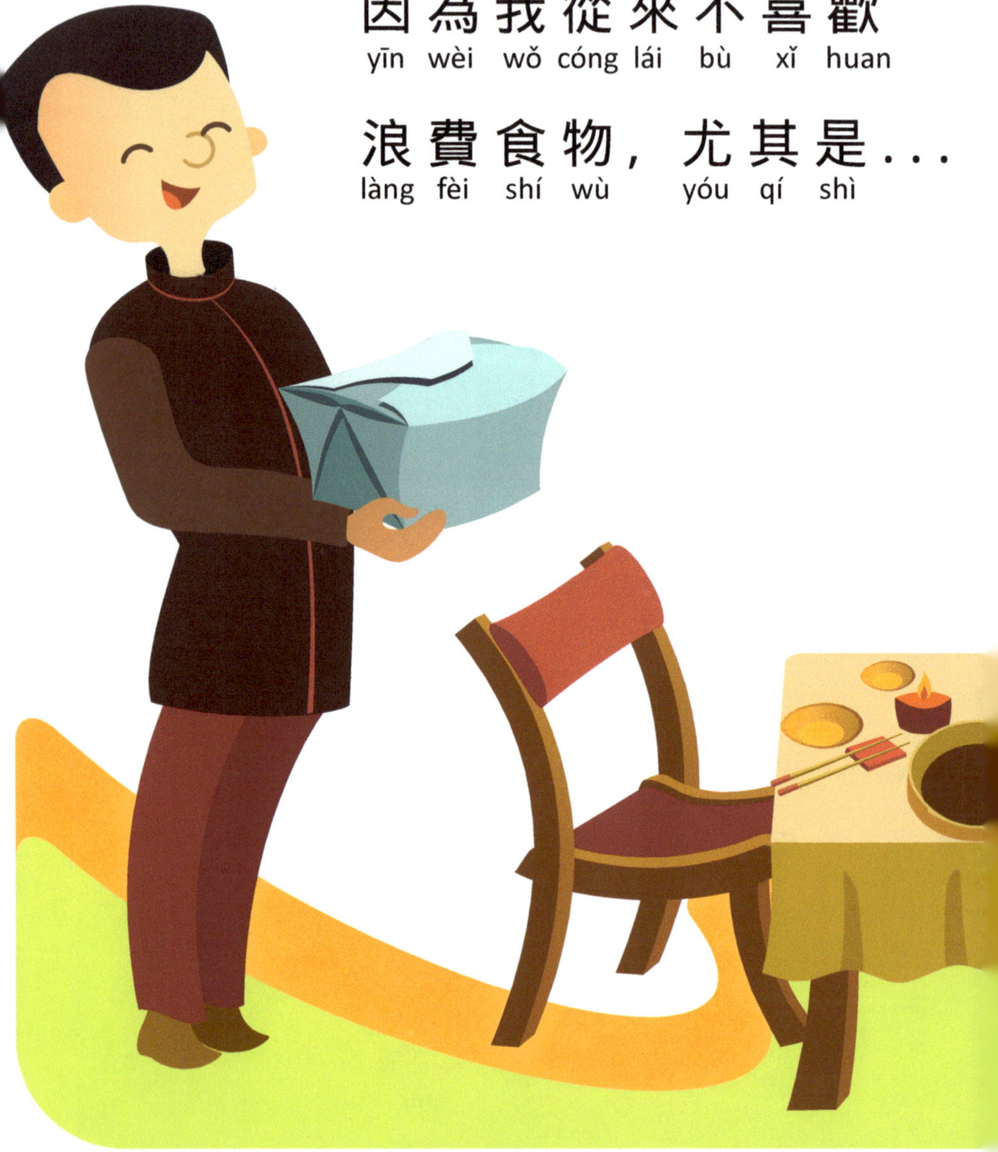

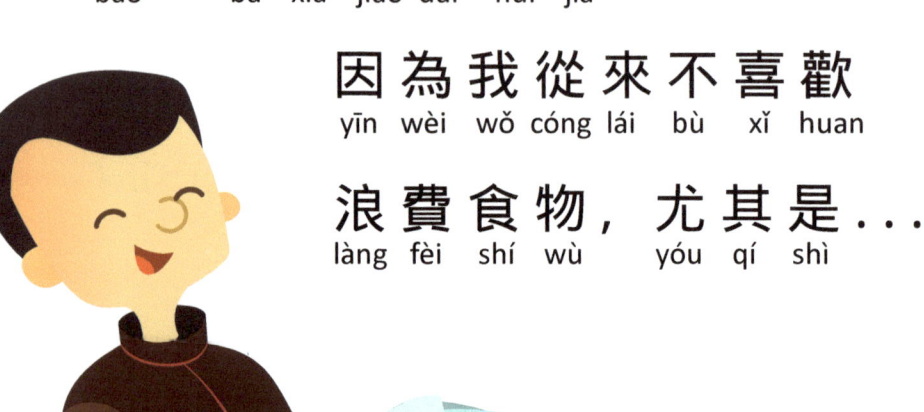

So I ask the waiter for a box and take the Har Gao's home.

Because I never like to waste food especially when it's ...

蝦餃！
xiā jiǎo

蝦餃！蝦餃！
xiā jiǎo　　xiā jiǎo

我愛蝦餃
wǒ ài xiā jiǎo

# Har Gao!

**Har Gao! Har Gao!
I love my Har Gao!**